A Kid's Book of Experiments With

STARS

SURPRISING Science Experiments

Robert Gardner
and
Joshua Conklin

Enslow Publishing
101 W. 23rd Street
Suite 240
New York, NY 10011
USA

enslow.com

Published in 2016 by Enslow Publishing, LLC
101 W. 23rd Street, Suite 240, New York, NY 10011

Library of Congress Cataloging-in-Publication Data

Gardner, Robert.
A kid's book of experiments with stars / by Robert Gardner and Joshua Conklin.
p. cm.—(Surprising science experiments)
Includes bibliographical references and index.
ISBN 978-0-7660-7270-1 (library binding)
ISBN 978-0-7660-7268-8 (pbk.)
ISBN 978-0-7660-7269-5 (6-pack)
1. Astronomy — Experiments — Juvenile literature. 2. Astronomy — Observations — Juvenile literature. 3. Science—Experiments — Juvenile literature. 4. Science projects — Juvenile literature. I. Gardner, Robert, 1929-. II. Conklin, Joshua. II. Title.
QB46.G3294 2016
520.78—d23

Printed in the United States of America

To Our Readers: We have done our best to make sure all website addresses in this book were active and appropriate when we went to press. However, the author and the publisher have no control over and assume no liability for the material available on those websites or on any websites they may link to. Any comments or suggestions can be sent by e-mail to customerservice@enslow.com.

Photo Credits: Throughout book: Sapann-Design/Shutterstock.com (colorful alphabet), Login/Shutterstock.com (series logo), Wiktoria Pawlak/Shutterstock.com (lightbulb), VLADGRIN/Shutterstock.com (science background), Aleksandrs Bondars/Shutterstock.com (banners), vector-RGB/Shutterstock.com (arrows); cover, p. 1 Eileen Hart/E+/Getty Images (boy with telescope); p. 4 AstroStar/Shutterstock.com; p. 21 NASA/SDO/HMI; p. 23 Tomruen/Wikimedia Commons/Lunar_eclipse_oct_8_2014_Minneapolis_4_46am.png/public domain; p. 30 SrsPvl/Shutterstock.com; p. 39 NASA; p. 44 NASA/SDO.

Illustration Credit: Accurate Art, Inc. c/o George Barile.

CONTENTS

Introduction

Have you ever been outside on a clear night, looked up at the stars, and dreamed about what's out there beyond the reach of humankind? The billions of stars in the universe have inspired the minds of scientists and the imaginations of artists for centuries. An entire branch of science—astronomy—is devoted to the study of celestial objects such as stars. This book will not offer all the answers to the Cosmos; however, you will learn more about the stars, the constellations they form, and how they move across the sky. You'll discover more about some of Earth's closest celestial neighbors, the sun and the moon. Let's get to work!

Two Constellations and a Direction

Sir John Frederick William Herschel, a nineteenth-century astronomer, said, "The stars are the landmarks of they universe." For centuries, sailors and travelers relied upon the stars and constellations as nighttime navigational points. A constellation is a collection of stars that form a pattern. Many cultures imagined that these patterns formed figures from mythology. For example, the constellation Orion is a representation of a giant huntsman in Greek mythology. Modern astronomers list eighty-eight constellations and, like sailors of old, we can use two of them to help find a direction. Let's get started.

Experiment 1: The Big Dipper, the Little Dipper, and a Direction

Things You Will Need:

- an adult
- clear, dark night
- open area
- flashlight or lantern
- hammer
- 2 stakes or sticks
- compass (optional)

If you live in the northern hemisphere, including the United States and Canada, you can see the "Big Dipper" and the "Little Dipper" in the northern sky. These two well-recognized figures are actually asterisms, or parts of the larger constellations Ursa Major (Larger She-Bear) and Ursa Minor (Smaller She-Bear) respectively. On a clear, dark night, you can see them easily.

1. When it is dark and not very cloudy, go outside. **Ask an adult** to come with you (at least this first time).

2. Find an open area and locate the northern sky. (You can use a compass if you have one.)

3. Look for a group of stars arranged like the ones at the bottom of Figure 1. (Use your flashlight or lantern to reference the book, then turn it off and look back at the sky.) These stars form the Big Dipper. Because constellations appear to turn over time (we'll learn more about that later), it may not look exactly like the drawing. If you rotate the figure in your hands you can see how it might appear in the sky. The Big Dipper's stars are bright so you should be able to find them easily.

4. The Little Dipper is not as easy to spot but you can use the pointer stars of the Big Dipper, Merak and Dubhe, to help.

Figure 1

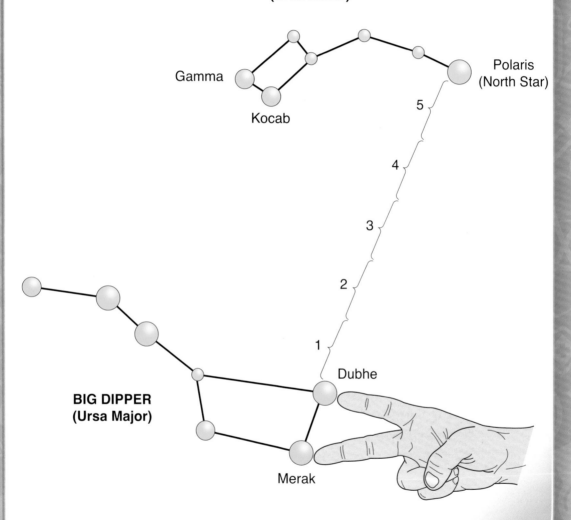

LITTLE DIPPER
(Ursa Minor)

Gamma

Kocab

Polaris
(North Star)

5

4

3

2

1

Dubhe

BIG DIPPER
(Ursa Major)

Merak

The Big Dipper can direct you to Polaris (the North Star) and the Little Dipper.

Extend your arm. Put your first two fingers on the pointer stars. Keeping your fingers that distance apart, move them in the direction given by the pointer stars. The distance from the Big Dipper to the North Star (Polaris) is about five times the distance between your fingers.

Polaris is a relatively dim star at the end of the Little Dipper's handle. Follow the handle and you should discover the rest of Little Dipper. Sometimes the Little Dipper may appear to be pouring water into the Big Dipper, or vice versa.

The North Star (Polaris) is almost directly above Earth's North Pole. This makes it a handy guide when you are looking to find which way is north.

5. Have a partner stand a few meters (yards) north of you under your sight line to form a line that appears beneath Polaris.

Drive a stake (or stick) into the ground where you are standing. Drive a second stake into the ground where your partner is standing. The two stakes should almost point toward the North Pole. Save this north-south line for future experiments.

Experiment 2: Can a Magnetic Compass Be Used to Find True North?

Things You Will Need:

- magnetic compass
- north-south line you made in Experiment 1

Many people think a magnetic compass needle always points toward the North Pole, otherwise known as true north. Let's check.

1. Find the north-pointing line (a line between the two stakes) you made in Experiment 1.

2. Hold a magnetic compass above the line that points toward true north. You will probably find that the compass needle is not parallel to the true-north line you made in Experiment 1. (If you live on a line between Florida's panhandle and Lake Superior's western shore the lines may be close to parallel.) Save this north-south line for future experiments.

Two Constellations and a Direction: An Explanation

The line you marked in Experiment 1 should point in a direction very close to true north. Polaris is less than one degree away from being over the North Pole.

A compass needle does not point toward Earth's North Pole. It points toward Earth's magnetic North Pole. That pole is located in Canada's Boothia Peninsula about 1,900 km (1,200 mi) from Earth's geographic North Pole. Unlike the geographic North Pole, the magnetic North Pole is not fixed; it moves.

If you live in the eastern United States, your compass needle should point west of true north. In the western United States, compass needles point east of true north.

IDEAS for a Science Project

- ○ Some scientists believe birds and other animals use Earth's magnetic field to guide them during migrations. What evidence is there to support this idea?

- ○ If you lived south of the equator, how would you find true north at night?

- ○ How can you use the altitude of Polaris to find your latitude?

Finding and Watching the Polar Constellations

We learned in the previous experiment that constellations can help point us in a direction. If we look skyward at different times of night, will those stars remain in the same place? We can use the polar constellations (those constellations found near Polaris) to discover if the stars move through the sky at night. Figure 2 shows the polar constellations as they appear in mid-September around 9 p.m. (the exact time will vary depending on your time zone). So do the stars remain fixed in the sky or do they appear to move? Let's find out!

Experiment 3: Observing the Polar Constellations Over Time

Things You Will Need:

- adult permission
- clear sky
- good visibility
- alarm clock
- notebook and pencil
- flashlight or lantern
- compass (optional)

Figure 2

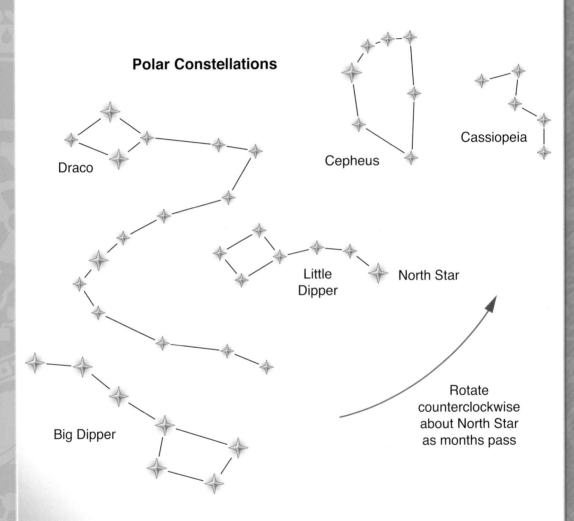

Polar Constellations

Draco

Cepheus

Cassiopeia

Little
Dipper

North Star

Big Dipper

Rotate
counterclockwise
about North Star
as months pass

The polar constellations look like this at about 9 p.m. in mid–September.

1. Examine Figure 2, which shows the major polar constellations.

2. On a clear, dark night see if you can locate them. Many think Cassiopeia looks like a dentist's chair, some see Cepheus as a kite, and Draco is often called a dragon. In the southern part of the United States, the polar constellations will not be completely visible all the time. Further south, at the equator, Polaris would be on the horizon.

3. Observe the polar constellations, especially the Big Dipper and Cassiopeia, soon after dark. Make a drawing of their appearance in the sky.

4. With **adult permission**, set your alarm clock for an early morning hour before dawn. Get up and observe the polar constellations again. What do you find? Has the position of the constellations changed? If so, how?

Observing the Polar Constellations Over Time in Months

You observed what happened to the polar constellations over an evening. Will we see a similar phenomenon over months? Ask permission to stay up long enough to observe the polar constellations on a clear night at least once a month and watch what happens!

1. On your first night, draw a picture of the Big Dipper as you see it around 9:30 p.m.

2. Make new drawings of the Big Dipper at about the same time about a month later.

3. Repeat the same procedure for a few more months. What can you conclude?

Finding and Watching the Polar Constellations: An Explanation

During one night, you saw the polar constellations appear to change their positions in the sky. They appear to turn slowly counterclockwise around Polaris. Polaris is almost directly above Earth's North Pole and its position is nearly fixed.

You may have realized why the polar constellations appear to move. Earth rotates on its axis a full 360 degrees every 24 hours, so the constellations appear to turn the opposite direction of Earth. They too appear to turn 360 degrees every 24 hours.

Over the course of months you also observed changes in the sky. Earth makes one orbit about the sun every 365.25 days. As Earth moves along its orbit, the sky and stars we see change.

Figure 3 shows the appearance of the Big Dipper at 9 p.m. in the middle of the month during an entire year. You hopefully found something similar during your investigation.

Notice in Figure 3 that the line drawn across the pointer stars moves like a clock hand turning backward. In January, the line is at three o'clock, in February, it is at two o'clock, in March it is at one o'clock, and so on. The constellations appear to move counterclockwise during the year because Earth moves around the sun in the opposite direction.

Figure 3

JANUARY
(3 o'clock at 9 P.M.)

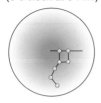

FEBUARY
(2 o'clock at 9 P.M.)

MARCH
(1 o'clock at 9 P.M.)

APRIL
(12 o'clock at 9 P.M.)

MAY
(11 o'clock at 9 P.M.)

JUNE
(10 o'clock at 9 P.M.)

JULY
(9 o'clock at 9 P.M.)

AUGUST
(8 o'clock at 9 P.M.)

SEPTEMBER
(7 o'clock at 9 P.M.)

OCTOBER
(6 o'clock at 9 P.M.)

NOVEMBER
(5 o'clock at 9 P.M.)

DECEMBER
(4 o'clock at 9 P.M.)

The drawings show the position of the Big Dipper's pointer stars at approximately 9 p.m. at the middle of each month. Notice that a line along the pointer stars and beyond turns counterclockwise as months pass. It moves back one hour each month when seen at 9 p.m. standard time.

Experiment 4: A Constellation to Watch Each Season

Things You Will Need:

- A clear night
- compass (optional)
- flashlight or lantern (optional)
- an adult or friend (optional)

Ancient astronomers believed that Earth was the center of the universe and that the stars, including our sun, revolved around Earth every day. We know now that Earth orbits the sun. This orbit causes the sky we see at night to change during the year (see Figure 4).

As Figure 4 shows, the sky, stars, and constellations we see change from season to season. Below, we suggest one major constellation to observe each season. However, if you enjoy finding constellations, you can find many more using a star chart. There is a website with links to star charts in the **Learn More** section of this book. Several major constellations for each season are shown in Figure 5. This is a fun activity to do with **an adult** or friend!

Figure 4

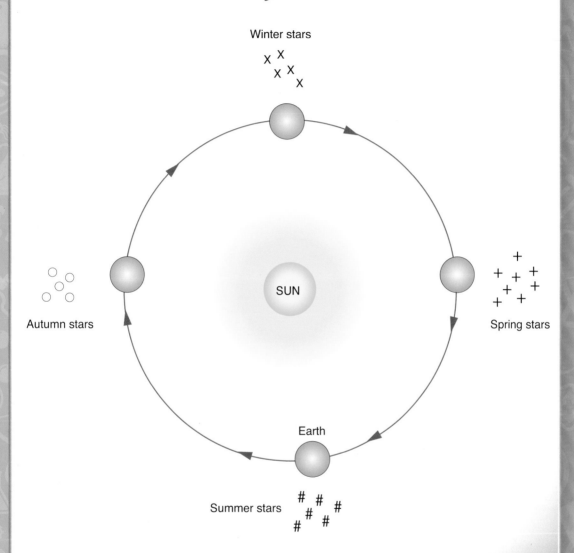

Winter stars

Autumn stars

SUN

Spring stars

Earth

Summer stars

Because Earth revolves around the sun, our view of the stars changes. The stars we see at different seasons are represented by os, xs, +s, and #s. The sun and other stars move very little. Earth moves a lot. The sky and its stars change because we see different parts of the sky as we revolve beneath it.

Figure 5

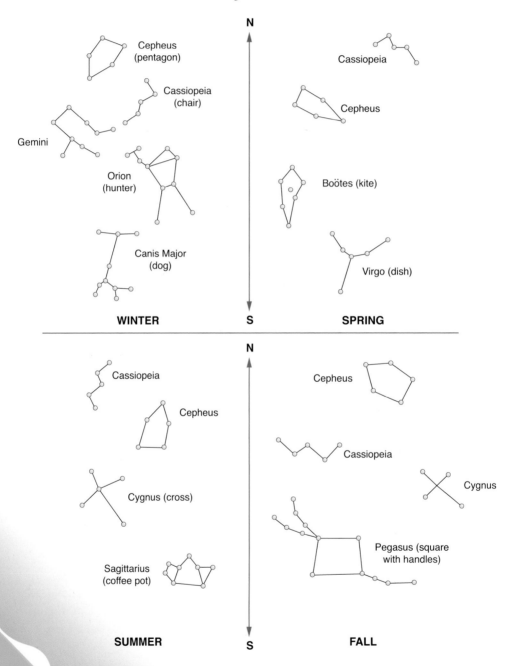

The visible constellations change with the seasons.

A Winter Constellation: Orion

Orion's bright stars are easily seen in the winter sky. During the evening in December and January, you can see Orion by looking south or southeast high in the sky. Orion is one of the more easily recognizable constellations and visible in night skies across the globe. The earliest depiction of Orion was found in a cave in Germany and estimated to be over 32,000 years old! Orion's name comes from the Greek legend of a supernaturally strong hunter, but the constellation is also a part of Chinese and Middle Eastern lore.

You'll be able to watch Orion through the winter and into the spring. In which direction does it seem to move as weeks and months pass? What other constellations can you find in these months with your star chart?

A Spring Constellation: Boötes

In early spring the constellation Boötes can be seen quite high in the eastern or southeastern sky. It has a warped-kite shape and contains the fourth brightest star in the night sky—Arcturus. The name Boötes was first used in the famous book by Homer, *The Odyssey*, as a point of navigation. Boötes is close to the Big Dipper and the sky's second largest constellation, Virgo. What other constellations can you see in the spring sky?

A Summer Constellation: Sagittarius

The coffee pot shape of Sagittarius is easy to find in the southern sky. Sagittarius is often depicted as a centaur, a half-man half-horse creature of Greek legend. The constellation is near one of the more dense parts of the Milky Way, the galaxy that is home to our solar system. Use your star chart to further explore the summer sky.

A Fall Constellation: Cygnus

Cygnus, which can be found in the western sky, is known as "the swan," but also contains the notable asterism (a collection of stars usually smaller than a constellation) known as the Northern Cross. The Kepler spacecraft launched by NASA has located many planets in the Cygnus star system. One such planet, Kepler-22b, is believed to be most likely to contain extraterrestrial life! Other constellations to look for are Auriga high in the east, and Cepheus and Cassiopeia to the north.

Earth's Star

So far we have searched for stars in the night sky. However, there is one star you will have no trouble seeing during the day. This star, the one closest to Earth, is the sun! It is 150 million kilometers (93 million miles) from Earth. That may seem like a long way but the next nearest star is Proxima Centauri, 4.27 light-years away. A light-year is the distance light travels in one year. Since light travels at a speed of about 300,000 km (186,000 mi) per second, the distance to Proxima Centauri is the speed of light times 60 s/min x 60 min/hr x 24 hr/d x 365 d/yr x 4.27, which equals about 40 trillion kilometers or about 24 trillion miles! The nighttime stars don't go away during the day but when the sun is visible, it is difficult to see other stars. The sun's brightness outshines the dimmer light from more distant stars.

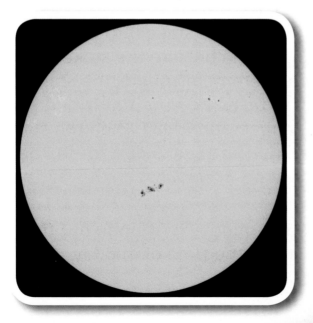

The sun is our closest star. Sunspots are places where gases are cooler than the other surrounding gases.

Experiment 5: Using a Shadow to Find North

Things You Will Need:

- **an adult**
- **open, level, sunny area**
- **stake**
- **hammer**
- **carpenter's level**
- **local newspaper or Internet**
- **watch or clock**

In Experiment 1 you found the direction of true north using the star Polaris. There is another way to find true north using the sun's shadow.

1. Find an open, level ground where the sun shines most of the day.

2. With **an adult's** help, drive a stake into the ground. Use a carpenter's level to be sure the stake is vertical. In the northern hemisphere, the stake's shadow will be shortest when the sun is due south. This will happen at midday when the sun is highest in the sky. If the sun is due south, the shadow it casts will point toward true north (the North Pole).

3. You might think that midday is at noon but this is seldom true. To find the time of midday, use

the time of sunrise and sunset. This information will be in your local paper or on the Internet. For example, on June 26, 2015, the sun rose at 5:06 a.m. and set at 8:21 p.m. Midday is halfway between those two times.

The total time between sunrise and sunset was fourteen hours and seventy-five minutes. Midday was at half that time: seven hours and thirty-seven and a half minutes after sunrise. So midday was at 5:06 + 7:37.5 = 12:43.5 p.m. (You may want **an adult** to help you with the math to find midday.)

4. At midday, the stake's shadow will be shortest and will point toward true north. Place a second stake at the end of the first stake's shadow. The two stakes provide a line that gives the direction of true north. If you walked in that direction long enough you would arrive at the North Pole!

5. Save this north-south line for future experiments.

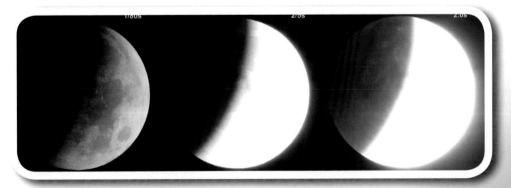

During this lunar eclipse, a huge shadow was cast by Earth on the moon. Notice that it shows Earth's curvature. What light source do you think cast the shadow?

Experiment 6: Where Does the Sun Rise and Set?

Things You Will Need:

- north-south line established in Experiment 5
- clear sky
- newspaper or Internet
- carpenter's square or board
- hammer
- 2 stakes

You have probably heard that the sun rises in the east and sets in the west. Is this always true? Let's find out.

1. Find the north-south line you established in Experiment 5.

2. Use that line to make an east-west line. An east-west line will be perpendicular to the north-south line. A large carpenter's square or a big square board may be helpful.

3. Drive stakes into the ground at the ends of the east-west line. Their shadows will help you determine the direction of the rising sun without having to look at it. (**Looking at the sun can damage your eyes.**)

4. Find the time of sunrise from a newspaper or the Internet.

5. With **an adult's permission** get up a few minutes before sunrise. Go to the east-west line you built. Watch the stakes' shadows as the sun rises. Did the sun rise due east? North of east? South of east?

6. Repeat the procedure at sunset. What was the direction of sunset?

7. Repeat this experiment every month. What can you conclude?

The Sun's Path as Seen on Earth

The sun rises, crosses the sky, and sets. To us, it looks as if it is moving. However, we know the sun only appears to move because Earth rotates (turns on its axis) as it revolves around the sun.

When you look at the sky, you see a dome filled with stars, clouds, or a clear blue surface. The sun seems to move east to west across that dome every day if you live below the Arctic Circle.

Astronomers call the dome we see the celestial hemisphere. A person on the opposite side of Earth sees the other celestial hemisphere. You can map the sun's path across this hemisphere in the next experiment.

Experiment 7:
The Sun's Path Across the Sky

Things You Will Need:

- clear sky
- clear plastic dome or a large fine-mesh kitchen strainer (domes can be found on some squirrel-proof bird feeders; science supply companies sell them as part of a globe kit)
- board or sheet of heavy cardboard
- pencil
- marking pen
- tape
- clock or watch
- round-headed map pins (if you use a strainer)
- yarn (if you use a strainer)

1. Begin shortly after sunrise. Put the dome or strainer on a level board or sheet of heavy cardboard. The dome or strainer represents the celestial hemisphere or sky. Use a pencil to trace the outer circumference of the dome or strainer on the board. (See Figure 6b.)

2. Remove the dome or strainer. Mark the center of the circle with a black dot. The dot represents your place under the celestial hemisphere.

Figure 6

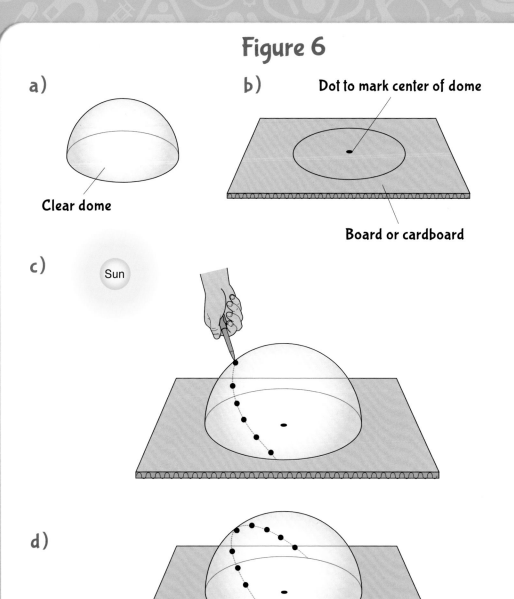

a)

Clear dome

b)

Dot to mark center of dome

Board or cardboard

c)

Sun

d)

a) Use a dome or strainer to mark the sun's path across the sky.
b) Mark the center of the dome with a dot. c) Use a marking pen
to map the sun's position in the sky. The shadow of the pen's
tip should fall on the dot at the center of the dome or strainer.
d) By the end of the day you will have a map of the sun's path.

3. Put the dome or strainer back in its original position. Tape it to the board or cardboard base. Be sure the base is level.

4. **If you use a clear dome**, chart the sun's position with a marking pen. Place the pen's tip on the dome so that the tip's shadow is on the dot at the dome's center. Mark that spot on the dome. It maps the sun's position. (See Figure 6c.)

5. Mark the sun's position about every hour while the sun is above the horizon. By day's end, you will have a map of the sun's path (Figure 6d).

6. **If you use a strainer**, round-headed map pins can be used. Cast their shadows on the center dot and leave pins in the strainer at their various positions each hour. At the end of the day, you will have a map of the sun's path.

    Weave a piece of colored yarn through the pin positions as you remove the pins. You will then have a permanent record of the sun's path for that day.

7. Try to do this experiment at least four times. Do it around March 21, June 21, September 21, and December 21. In that way you will have the highest, lowest, and middle paths of the sun for an entire year.

    When is the sun's path highest and longest? When is its path shortest and lowest?

Experiment 8:
How Big Is the Sun?

Things You Will Need:

- shady tree
- sunny day
- a pin
- file cards
- tape
- meterstick or yardstick
- a partner
- ruler
- notebook and pen or pencil
- an adult (optional if you need help with the math)

If someone asked you to measure the sun, you might laugh. However, if you know our distance from the sun, you can make a good estimate of the sun's diameter. An ancient astronomer named Aristarchus made a good estimate of the distance to the sun. His method, which has been refined with better instruments, shows that the distance to the sun is approximately 150 million kilometers or 93 million miles. You can use that information to determine the sun's diameter.

These circles of light under a shade tree are called sun dapples.

1. Look under a shady tree on a sunny day. You will see circles filled with light. These are called sun dapples and are actually pinhole images of the sun.

2. You can make a pinhole image of the sun. Use a pin to make a small hole through the center of a file card.

3. Tape a second card to the end of a meterstick or yardstick (Figure 7a).

4. Use the second card as a screen to capture the sun's image.

Figure 7

a)

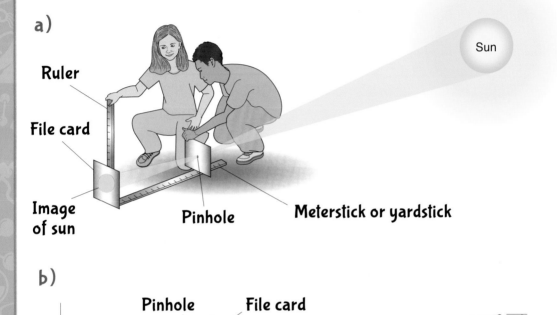

Ruler

File card

Image
of sun

Pinhole

Meterstick or yardstick

Sun

b)

Pinhole   File card

d

l

L

D

A pinhole, measurements, and a known distance to the sun
will enable you to calculate the sun's diameter.

5. Move the card with the pinhole along the stick as shown in Figure 7a. Make a sharp image of the sun on the card. Ask a partner to measure the diameter of the sun's image. What is the diameter of the image in centimeters (or inches)? Record the diameter.

6. Measure and record the distance between the image and the pinhole. Now you can calculate the sun's diameter.

7. Figure 7b shows two triangles. The smaller triangle has a base d (the diameter of the image). It has an altitude l, the distance from pinhole to image. The large triangle's apex is at the pinhole. Its altitude, L, is the distance to the sun. Its base, D, is the sun's diameter.

8. The two triangles are similar. This means their sides have the same ratio so:

$$\frac{D}{L} = \frac{d}{l} \quad \text{or} \quad D = \frac{d}{l} \times L$$

The sun's diameter, D, is equal to $d/l \times L$

When the authors did this experiment, they found the diameter of the sun's image to be 0.6 cm. The distance from pinhole to image, d, was 60 cm. Since the distance to the sun, L, is 150,000,000 km, the diameter of the sun, D, was:

$$\frac{0.6 \text{ cm}}{60 \text{ cm}} \times 150,000,000 \text{ km} = 1,500,000 \text{ km or } 900,000 \text{ mi}$$

The diameter of Earth is about 12,500 km or 7,800 mi. So, we calculated the sun's diameter to be about 115 times as large as Earth's. We were close, as it is actually 109 times as large.

Earth's Star: An Explanation

The sun rises due east and sets due west only twice each year at the spring and fall equinoxes, around March 21 and September 21. After the spring equinox, the sun rises north of due east and sets north of due west.

At the fall equinox, the sun is again moving along a path above the equator. After that equinox, it begins to rise south of due east and set south of due west.

You will find a globe helpful in understanding the sun's changing path as seen from Earth.

Mapping the sun's path across the sky revealed a path that is highest around June 21, at the summer solstice. Its lowest path occurs around December 21 at the winter solstice. Its path around March 21 and September 21 are the same. These are the dates of the spring and autumn equinoxes. At these times, the sun moves along a path directly above Earth's equator.

You were able to measure the diameter of the sun using a pinhole image, the distance to the sun, and a pair of similar triangles. Pretty cool!

IDEAS for a Science Project

- How can you explain the sun dapples you see under a shade tree on a sunny day?

- What happens if you make a second pinhole in the file card you used in Experiment 8? A third? Can you make an array of sun dapples?

- How did Aristarchus determine the distance between Earth and the sun?

- How much time does it take for light from the sun to reach Earth?

The Moon: Earth's Natural Satellite

Man has sent countless satellites into the sky to predict weather, provide communication, make maps, and carry out various other functions. Earth, however, has only one natural satellite, the moon. Earth may have only one natural satellite (Jupiter has at least sixty-three!) but the moon has been here long before humans were around to look up at the night sky. Let's learn some more about it.

Experiment 9: Watching the Moon

Things You Will Need:

- local newspaper or the Internet
- notebook
- pen or pencil
- calendar

You've probably noticed that the moon appears in different forms, from a large round globe to a thin crescent. First, let's observe how it changes and then figure out why it changes. Begin your explorations after a new moon (when the moon can't be seen from Earth).

1. Find the date of a new moon. A new moon occurs when the moon is between Earth and the sun. Your local newspaper or the Internet will give you the date of a new moon.

2. A day or two after a new moon, look for the moon immediately after sunset. You will see it as a bright crescent (sliver) in the western sky.

3. Make a drawing of that moon in a notebook. Record the date and time.

4. Continue to look for the moon right after sunset for the next two weeks. In your notebook, draw a picture of the moon that you see. Record the time and date. Also record the approximate distance, in degrees, between the setting sun and the moon. One fist at arm's length is approximately ten degrees. (See Figure 8.)

Figure 8

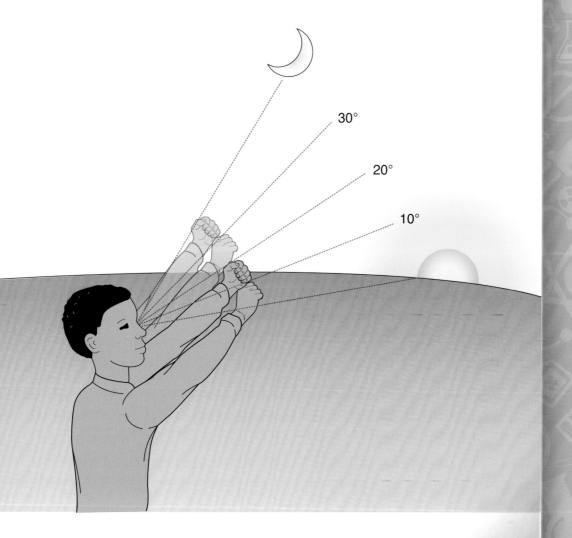

You can measure the angular distance between the sun and the moon using fists. One fist at arm's length is approximately ten degrees.

5. You will see the distance between the sun and the moon increasing. But is the moon still following the sun? Does it appear to move east to west after sunset? How is the moon's shape changing? Is the moon setting later as the days pass?

Your newspaper or the Internet will provide rising and setting times for both the sun and the moon.

6. Two weeks after a new moon, begin looking for a full moon at sunset. A full moon rises close to the time of sunset. Again, your local newspaper or the Internet will give you the date of a full moon.

7. After a full moon, continue to look for the moon. Look just before and after sunrise and during the day. When you see the moon, record it in your notebook. Record what you see and where you see it. Is the moon now east or west of the sun? Is its angular distance from the sun increasing or decreasing?

8. Continue to watch the moon for several months. Are you beginning to see a pattern to its motion and changing appearance? How much time passes between full moons? Can you explain the moon's changing shape?

9. Try to make a model of the moon and sun. The model should explain the moon's changing appearance. It should also explain why the separation between the sun and moon changes.

The moon's surface is covered with craters. This photo shows the moon's Aitken Crater. What do you think made the craters? Why doesn't Earth's surface have as many craters?

Experiment 10:
A Model to Explain the Moon's Changing Appearance

Things You Will Need:

- white Styrofoam ball 5–10 cm (2–4 in) in diameter mounted on a toothpick or a suitable substitute such as a white tennis ball on a plastic pill bottle
- early sunny morning or late afternoon sun or single bright lightbulb in a dark room

You have seen the moon's apparent shape change from one new moon to the next. Were you able to design a model to explain what you saw? If you did, compare your model with the one described in this experiment.

1. In this model, your head represents Earth. The ball represents the moon. The sun or a lightbulb represents the sun.

2. Hold the ball at arm's length with your back to the sun (or lightbulb). The ball should be fully lit (Figure 9). You are looking at a model of a "full moon." We will assume that the moon orbits Earth.

Figure 9

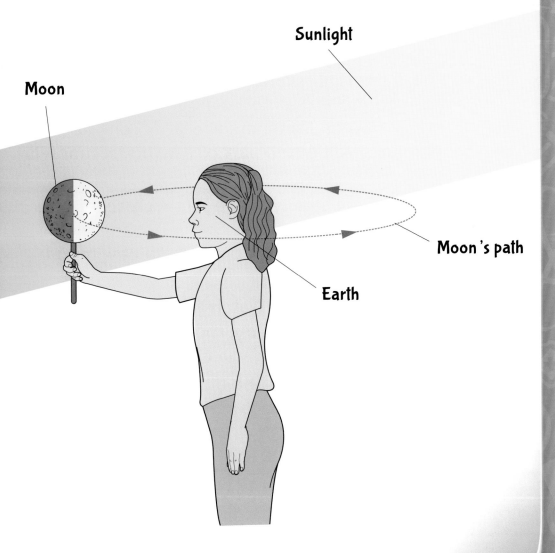

Sunlight

Moon

Moon's path

Earth

Use a model to show how the moon's shape appears to change from one full moon to the next.

3. Slowly turn to the left keeping the "moon" at arm's length and in the light. Watch the illuminated part of the moon. See it slowly shrink and become a half moon (last quarter). Continue to turn and see it become a crescent. Protect your eyes from the light from the real sun (or lightbulb) with your free hand as you move the model moon to a new moon position (between Earth and the sun). Look at the model moon. No lighted part of the model moon is now visible.

4. Continue to turn slowly to the left. A crescent (sliver) of moon will be seen. It models the moon you saw at sunset a day or two after a new moon in Experiment 9.

5. Continue to slowly turn. Watch the lit part of the moon increase until half the moon is lit (a first quarter moon).

6. Continue to slowly turn. The lighted part of the moon increases until it again becomes a full moon. The model has shown how a full lunar cycle takes place from one full moon to the next.

7. A good model should agree with what we find in the real world. Is this model a good one?

Earth's Natural Satellite: An Explanation

You observed the moon for several months and saw its shape grow from a crescent to a full moon then back to a crescent that was turned the opposite way.

The model showed the same lunar phases—crescent, first quarter, full moon, third quarter, and finally new moon. The model assumed that the moon orbits Earth. That assumption led to a model that agreed with your observations of the real moon's monthly journey.

Ancient astronomers assumed that both the sun and the moon, as well as all the stars and planets, orbited Earth. They were only right about the moon. Since the model worked, we can be quite sure the moon does orbit Earth. The time from one new moon to the next averages twenty-nine and a half days.

IDEAS for a Science Project

- Use the moon model to represent an eclipse of the moon (a lunar eclipse).

- Design and build a model of your own to show how the moon's appearance changes.

- Build a scale model of Earth and the moon. Use it to show why a lunar eclipse doesn't occur every month.

- Build a scale model of Earth, sun, and moon. Use it to show why solar eclipses do not occur every month.

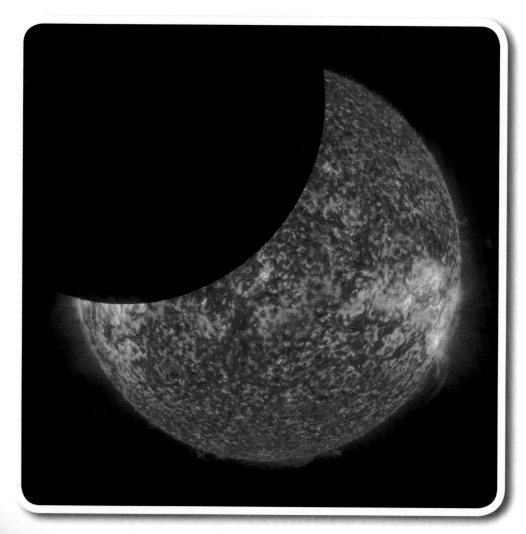

An eclipse of the sun occurs when the moon blocks light coming from the sun. At what phase of the moon would this happen?

Congratulations, astronomer. You've learned a lot about the stars, the constellations they form, and why they appear to move across the sky. You also explored Earth's star and our one natural satellite, the moon. If you enjoyed your trip through the stars, you can learn more about the world around you by taking a look at the other books in this series, which investigate color, light, animals, sound, and time. Keep learning, scientist!

GLOSSARY

astronomer—Someone who studies stars, other celestial bodies, and the universe as a whole.

celestial—Relating to the sky or part of the sky.

circumference—A measurement of the distance around something.

constellation—A grouping of stars as seen from Earth. There are eighty-eight modern constellations.

diameter—The length of a straight line passing through the center of a circle and connecting two points on the circle's circumference.

equinox—When the sun crosses the Earth along the equator and night and day are of equal length. There is both a spring and fall equinox.

hemisphere—A half of the earth, usually divided into northern and southern halves by the equator, or into western and eastern halves by an imaginary line passing through the poles.

light-year—A unit of measurement that represents the distance light travels in one year in a vacuum, or about 5.88 trillion miles.

parallel—Two or more lines are parallel if they would continue forever without crossing.

perpendicular—Lines that are at right angles to one another.

polar—Something is considered polar if it exists at or near one of the geographic poles or is within the Arctic or Antarctic circles.

revolution—One trip around an orbit. Earth's orbit around the sun takes 365.25 days, or one year.

rotation—The act of turning on a central point or axis.

LEARN MORE

Books

Fox, Karen. *Older Than the Stars.* Watertown, MA: Charlesbridge, 2011.

Hughes, Catherine D. *National Geographic Kids First Big Book of Space.* Washington, DC: National Geographic Kids, 2012.

Sisson, Stephanie. *Star Stuff: Carl Sagan and the Mysteries of the Cosmos.* New York: Roaring Book Press, 2014.

Websites

Ducksters
ducksters.com/science/star.php
A simple and interesting introduction to stars.

NASA Kids' Club
http://www.nasa.gov/audience/forkids/kidsclub/ flash/index.html#.Vae5-0YnWNc
Facts, games, and puzzles will entertain you and teach you more about stars.

Science Kids
sciencekids.co.nz/sciencefacts/space/stars.html
Lots of facts about stars with a collection of links.

Sky Maps
skymaps.com/downloads.html
Find PDF downloads of star charts for your location.

INDEX